THE
OK OF...

D1372315

WHICH?

KINGFISHER
NEW YORK

KINGFISHER
LONDON & NEW YORK

Copyright © Kingfisher 2011
Published in the United States by Kingfisher,
175 Fifth Ave., New York, NY 10010
Kingfisher is an imprint of Macmillan
Children's Books, London.
All rights reserved.

Distributed in the U.S. by Macmillan, 175 Fifth Ave.,
New York, NY 10010

Illustrated by Ray Bryant
Concept by Jo Connor

Library of Congress Cataloging-in-Publication data
has been applied for.

ISBN 978-0-7534-6599-8

Kingfisher books are available for special promotions and
premiums. For details contact: Special Markets Department,
Macmillan, 175 Fifth Ave., New York, NY 10010.

For more information, please visit www.kingfisherbooks.com

Printed in China
10 9 8 7 6 5 4 3 2 1
TTR/0511/LFG/UNTD/140MA

WHAT'S IN THIS BOOK?

WHICH...

HAVE YOU EVER ASKED YOURSELF WHICH?

It's only natural to be confused by the world around us . . . It is a very complicated and surprising place sometimes! And you'll never understand what's going on around you unless you ask yourself "WHICH?" every now and then.

"Which" is what this book is all about.

We have traveled over the land, under the sea, up mountains, across deserts—and even into outer space—to collect up as many tricky questions as we could find . . .

. . . and we also found the answers for you!

We now invite you to come with us on our journey around the world of "WHICH" so that we can show you all the answers we discovered.

Did you know . . .

Many cave animals are blind. They do not need sight because they live in total darkness.

While we were searching for all those answers, we found out some other pretty interesting things, too. We wrote them all down on these panels—so you can memorize these facts and impress your friends!

We also thought it might be fun to see how much of this shiny new knowledge you can remember—so at the back of the book, on pages 56 and 57, you'll find some Quick-Quiz questions to test you out. It's not as scary as it sounds—we promise it'll be fun. (And besides, we've given you all the answers on pages 58 and 59.)

Are you ready for this big adventure? Then let's go!

QUICK-QUIZ QUESTIONS

WHICH IS THE HOTTEST PLANET?

Did you know . . .

Venus is covered by clouds of gas that act like a big blanket, keeping in the Sun's heat.

Venus is the hottest planet, even though Mercury is closer to the Sun. The temperature on Venus can reach 930°F (500°C)—that is eight times hotter than it gets in the Sahara (a desert)—the hottest place on Earth.

WHICH IS THE COLDEST PLANET?

Did you know . . .

Pluto used to be known as the coldest planet. Then, in 2006, scientists decided that it was too small to count as a planet. Now, Pluto is called a dwarf planet instead.

Neptune is the coldest planet. It is about 30 times farther from the Sun than Earth is. Temperatures on Neptune can get as low as -330°F (-200°C). Neptune is also the planet with the fastest winds—they whip around at 1,340 miles (2,160 kilometers) per hour.

WHICH BIRD FLIES UNDERWATER?

Did you know...

Penguins cannot breathe underwater. Every few minutes, they come back to the surface to take in a breath of air.

Penguins cannot fly through the air because their wings are too short and stumpy. They are much more at home in the ocean, where they use their wings as flippers. They zip through the water, chasing fish and squids.

WHICH FISH HAS HEADLIGHTS?

Did you know . . .

Away from the shore, the ocean plunges to about 2.5 miles (4 kilometers) in most places. The deep sea is inky black, fridge cold—and home to some real oddballs!

The anglerfish lives in the dark depths of the ocean. It has a long fin dangling in front of its face. At the end of the fin is a blob that glows. Small fish are drawn to the light, only to disappear into the anglerfish's big, gaping mouth.

WHICH WAS THE BIGGEST DINOSAUR?

The biggest dinosaurs were the sauropods, a group of lumbering plant eaters that had very long necks. One of the biggest was a species of *Diplodocus* that measured 150 feet (45 meters) long and was taller than a four-story building.

Did you know...

Epidendrosaurus was one of the smallest-known dinosaurs. It was about the same size as a sparrow!

WHICH DINOSAUR HAD THOUSANDS OF TEETH?

Did you know . . .

Did you know . . .

Many hadrosaurs had a hollow head crest. The crest was probably used for display and may also have amplified a dinosaur's calls (made them louder).

Hadrosaurs had many tiny teeth in tightly packed rows. When these dinosaurs ground their top and bottom jaws together, their teeth worked like cheese graters. Hadrosaurs are sometimes called duck-billed dinosaurs, because of their beaklike snouts.

WHICH FROGS CAN FLY?

Did you know . . .

Tree frogs live in rainforests. Other forest gliders include the paradise flying snake and colugos, or flying lemurs.

Tree frogs can climb trees, and some types can even glide from one tree to another! These unusual frogs have big feet with long, webbed toes. When they spread their toes out, the webs of skin between them act like parachutes and help the frogs glide.

WHICH ANIMAL HAS A MAGIC HORN?

In some countries, rhinoceros horn is thought to be magical and is ground up for medicines. Even though it is against the law to hunt rhinos, some people still do. This is because they get a lot of money for a rhino's horn.

Did you know . . .

On some nature reserves, rangers cut off the rhinos' horns. It does not hurt the rhinos, and it stops poachers from killing them.

WHICH SEEDS SAIL AWAY?

Coconut palms grow near the ocean, so the ripe coconuts often fall into the water. Protected by their hard shells, they float out to sea. Eventually, after several weeks or months, they wash up on a new beach, where they sprout and start to grow.

Did you know . . .

The double coconut palm, or coco-de-mer, grows on islands in the Indian Ocean. Its gigantic seeds weigh up to 44 pounds (20 kilograms) each—as much as a sack of potatoes!

WHICH PLANT GROWS THE FASTEST?

Bamboo is the world's fastest-growing plant. Some types can grow almost 3 feet (1 meter) per day. At that rate, they would reach the roof of a two-story house in a week! The largest bamboos tower 130 feet (40 meters) high. It is hard to believe that they belong to the same plant family as grass.

WHICH FORESTS HAVE THE TALLEST TREES?

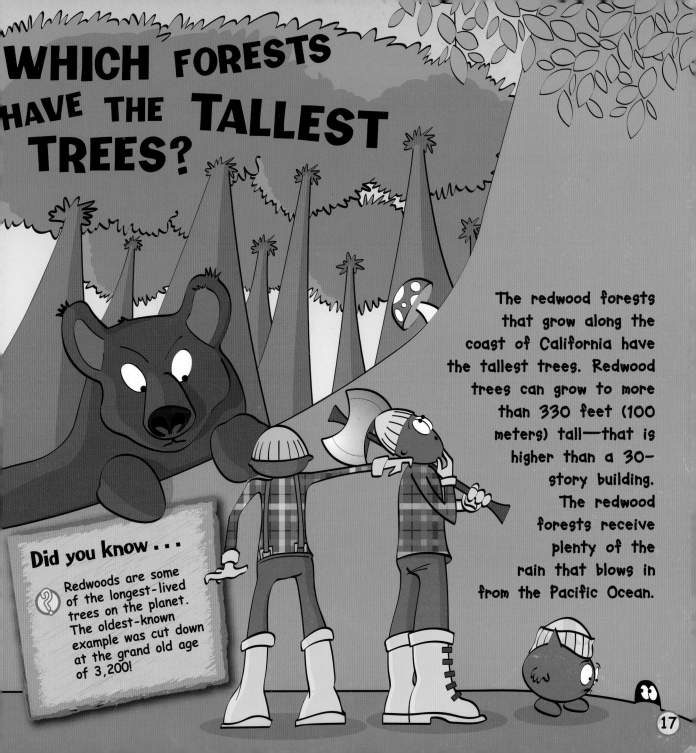

The redwood forests that grow along the coast of California have the tallest trees. Redwood trees can grow to more than 330 feet (100 meters) tall—that is higher than a 30-story building. The redwood forests receive plenty of the rain that blows in from the Pacific Ocean.

Did you know...

Redwoods are some of the longest-lived trees on the planet. The oldest-known example was cut down at the grand old age of 3,200!

WHICH PLANET IS KING?

18

Did you know . . .

Jupiter, Saturn, Uranus, and Neptune are the farthest planets from the Sun. All four are mostly made of gas, and they all have rings around them.

The planet Jupiter is named after the ancient Roman king of the gods. Jupiter is by far the biggest planet in our solar system, measuring more than 87,000 miles (140,000 kilometers) across. It is so big that it is 2.5 times the size of all of the other seven planets in the solar system added together.

WHICH IS THE RED PLANET?

Did you know . . .

Mars has the largest-known volcano in the solar system. Olympus Mons is 14 miles (22 kilometers) high and 430 miles (700 kilometers) across.

Mars, named after the Roman god of war, is often called the Red Planet. The ground there is covered in dusty red soil that gets swept up by the wind to make pink clouds! The rocks on Mars have a lot of iron in them, and iron turns red when it rusts. A better name for Mars might be the Rusty Planet.

WHICH IS THE SANDIEST DESERT?

Did you know . . .

The tallest sandcastle ever built stood more than 30 feet (9 meters) high—that is taller than five people standing on one another's shoulders!

The Sahara in North Africa is the largest hot desert in the world. Huge parts of it are covered with rolling hills of sand. Desert land is not always sandy, though. A lot of it is rocky or stony. Deserts are not always hot like the Sahara either. To count as desert, they just have to be very dry. The biggest one, overall, is Antarctica—a dry, cold desert continent.

WHICH RIVER WAS USED AS A ROAD?

Did you know . . .

The only farmland in Egypt was by the Nile. This was known as the Black Land, because when the river flooded, it left behind black mud.

The ancient Egyptians found the quickest way to get around was by using the Nile River. They built their boats out of reeds or wood. The boats were the only way to get from one side of the river to the other—unless you swam and liked crocodiles!

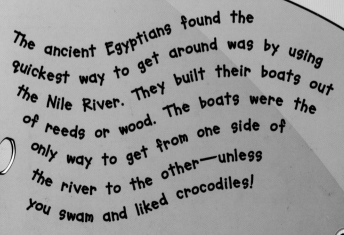

WHICH WAS THE DEEPEST DIVE?

Did you know...

In the deepest parts of the ocean, the water presses down so hard that it would feel like ten elephants sitting on top of you!

In 1960, two men dived almost 7 miles (11 kilometers) into the deepest-known part of the ocean, the Marianas Trench in the Pacific. They were inside one of the first submersibles, an incredibly strong craft called *Trieste*. It took them about five hours to reach the ocean floor.

WHICH IS THE BIGGEST OCEAN?

Did you know . . .

The Arctic is the smallest ocean—and also the coldest. For most of the year, it is covered in ice.

There are five oceans— the Pacific, the Atlantic, the Indian, the Arctic, and the Southern. The Pacific Ocean is by far the biggest. It is larger than the other four oceans put together and also much deeper. It covers about a third of Earth's surface.

23

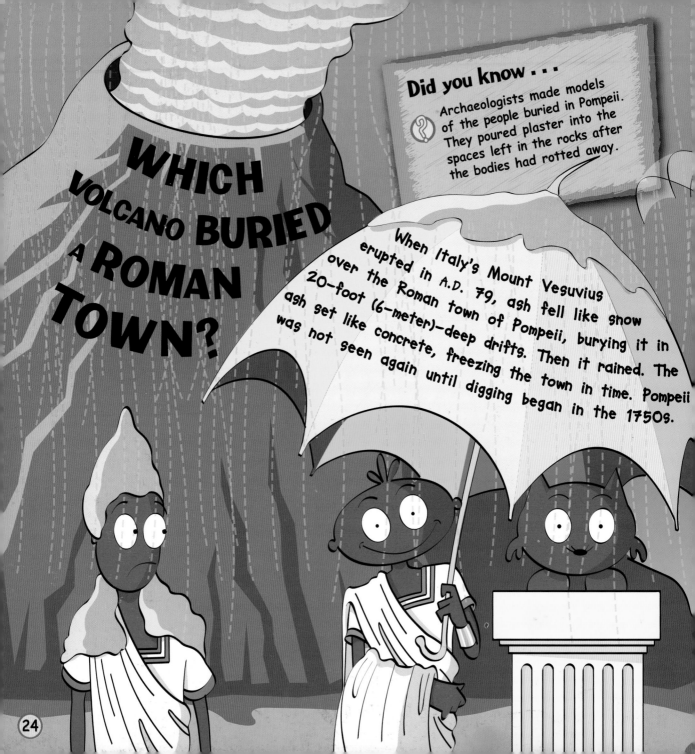

WHICH VOLCANO BURIED A ROMAN TOWN?

When Italy's Mount Vesuvius erupted in A.D. 79, ash fell like snow over the Roman town of Pompeii, burying it in 20-foot (6-meter)-deep drifts. Then it rained. The ash set like concrete, freezing the town in time. Pompeii was not seen again until digging began in the 1750s.

Did you know . . .

Archaeologists made models of the people buried in Pompeii. They poured plaster into the spaces left in the rocks after the bodies had rotted away.

WHICH BELLS MEASURE SOUNDS?

Did you know . . .

The blue whale is the loudest animal on Earth. Its underwater whistles measure as much as 188 decibels, which is louder than a space-rocket launch.

Sounds are measured in decibels. A very quiet sound, such as a whisper, is only 20 decibels, while the sound of church bells ringing measures 60 decibels. A jet plane taking off is about 140 decibels.

WHICH DINOSAURS HAD BODY ARMOR?

The thick, leathery skin on the top of *Ankylosaurus's* body had hard, bony lumps and spikes growing on it. This suit of body armor made the dinosaur into a living tank—very difficult to attack! Meat eaters would have broken their teeth if they had tried to bite into *Ankylosaurus's* skin.

WHICH ANIMALS HAVE SKELETONS ON THE OUTSIDE?

Not all animals have a skeleton inside them to hold their body together. Animals that do not have a skeleton are called invertebrates. Many invertebrates have a tough skin called an exoskeleton. This "outside skeleton" does the same job as an inside one. It protects and supports an animal's soft body.

WHICH PLANT FOOLS A FLY?

Did you know . . .

The Venus flytrap is a plant that springs a trap to catch its meal. Its hinged leaves snap shut if a fly brushes against one of their tiny, sensitive hairs.

Pitcher plants have jug-shaped leaves that tempt insects with a sugary smell. But the leaves are slippery traps. When a fly lands, it loses its footing, slips inside the "jug," and drowns in a pool of juice. Pitcher plants grow on boggy ground where the soil is poor. They need their juicy snacks for extra nourishment.

WHICH FLOWER FOOLS A BEE?

Did you know . . .

Many trees and grasses spread their pollen on the wind. They do not rely on animal visitors, so they do not need to grow colorful, sweet-smelling flowers in order to attract them.

A bee orchid's flowers look and smell just like female bees. Male bees zoom to the flowers, wanting to mate with them—but they have been tricked! The plant uses them as postal workers to deliver small packages of pollen to other orchids. When the pollen rubs off on another orchid, that flower can make seeds.

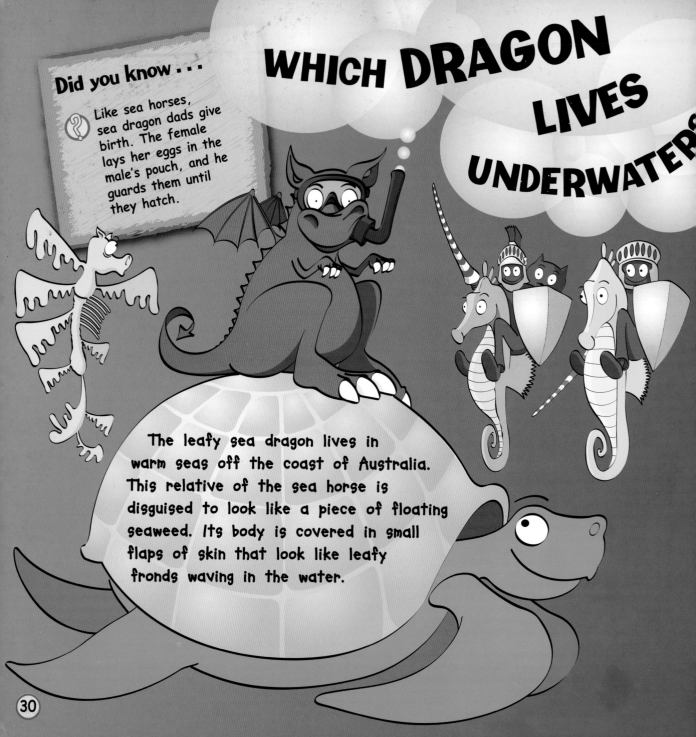

Did you know . . .

Like sea horses, sea dragon dads give birth. The female lays her eggs in the male's pouch, and he guards them until they hatch.

The leafy sea dragon lives in warm seas off the coast of Australia. This relative of the sea horse is disguised to look like a piece of floating seaweed. Its body is covered in small flaps of skin that look like leafy fronds waving in the water.

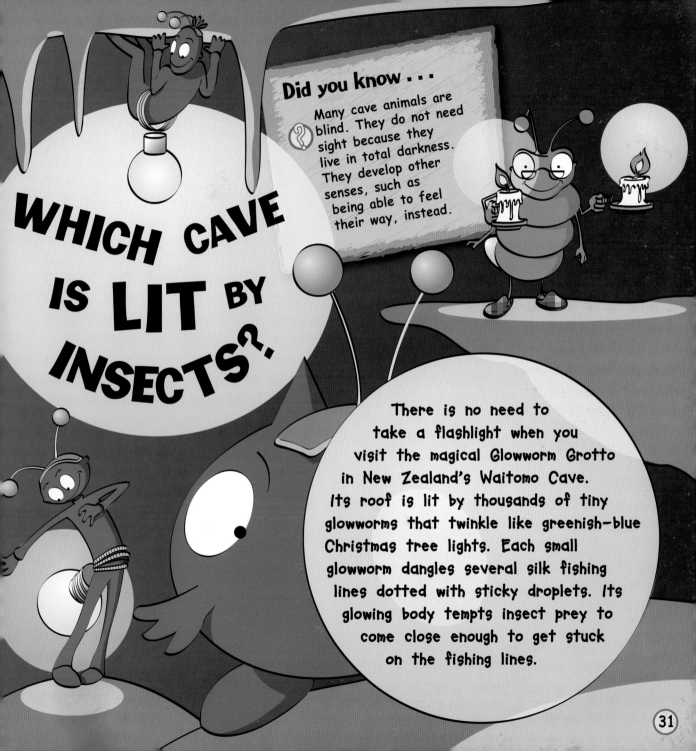

WHICH CAVE IS LIT BY INSECTS?

There is no need to take a flashlight when you visit the magical Glowworm Grotto in New Zealand's Waitomo Cave. Its roof is lit by thousands of tiny glowworms that twinkle like greenish-blue Christmas tree lights. Each small glowworm dangles several silk fishing lines dotted with sticky droplets. Its glowing body tempts insect prey to come close enough to get stuck on the fishing lines.

WHICH ANIMAL CHANGES COLOR?

Chameleons usually have brown-green skin, but it takes them only a few minutes to completely change their color. These strange little lizards can match their surroundings, which helps them hide from enemies. They also change color when they are frightened or angry. Chameleons watch out for danger with their amazing eyes, which swivel in different directions.

Did you know . . .

A chameleon catches its insect prey by shooting out its long, elastic tongue. The action is far too lightning fast for the human eye to follow.

WHICH ANIMALS ARE REPTILES?

Did you know . . .

The world's biggest reptile is the saltwater crocodile. This huge beast can grow to as long as 23 feet (7 meters) or longer.

Snakes, lizards, crocodiles, and turtles all belong to the same animal group—reptiles. All reptiles have a bony skeleton and scaly skin. Most of them lay eggs that hatch on land. But some reptiles give birth to live babies.

WHICH IS THE BIGGEST CREEPY-CRAWLY?

The Indonesian giant stick insect is the longest creepy-crawly in the world. At 13 inches (33 centimeters) long, it would only just fit inside the open pages of this book. The heavyweight champion of the insect world is the Goliath beetle. It weighs about the same as a hamster.

Did you know . . .

Long ago, before the age of the dinosaurs, monster dragonflies cruised through the air. Some were the size of seagulls.

WHICH IS THE SMALLEST CREEPY-CRAWLY?

Did you know . . .

There are almost one million known species of insects—but there may be as many as ten million more that we have not discovered yet.

You would find it hard to see a fairy fly, because it is no bigger than a period. Most species are only 0.2 millimeters long. This insect is actually a wasp, not a fly. The female lays her tiny eggs inside the eggs of other insects, such as cicadas and beetles.

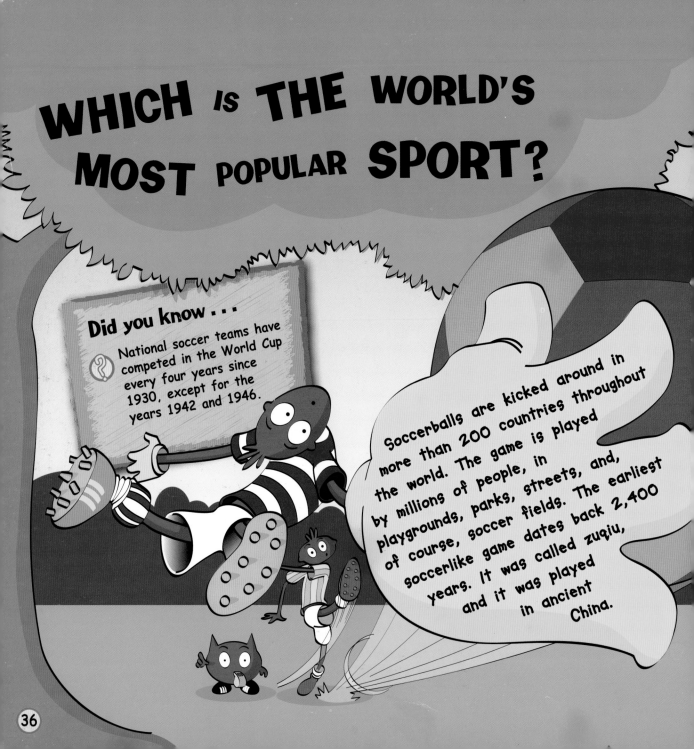

WHICH IS THE WORLD'S MOST POPULAR SPORT?

Did you know . . .

National soccer teams have competed in the World Cup every four years since 1930, except for the years 1942 and 1946.

Soccerballs are kicked around in more than 200 countries throughout the world. The game is played by millions of people, in playgrounds, parks, streets, and, of course, soccer fields. The earliest soccerlike game dates back 2,400 years. It was called zuqiu, and it was played in ancient China.

WHICH TOY IS MORE THAN 6,000 YEARS OLD?

Did you know . . .

Teddy bears are named after an American president, Theodore (Teddy) Roosevelt. Once, on a hunting trip, he came across a bear cub and refused to shoot it.

Dolls are the oldest toys of all. Children probably played with them in prehistoric times. Archaeologists have found carved wooden dolls from ancient Egypt, as well as the remains of Roman rag dolls. Dolls have been made from all sorts of materials, including fabric, wax, china, and plastic.

WHICH IS THE FASTEST CAR?

Did you know . . .

In 1899, a bullet-shaped electric car became the first-ever vehicle to travel faster than 60 miles (100 kilometers) per hour.

A British car called *Thrust SSC* set the world land-speed record in 1997. Using two jet aircraft engines in place of a normal car engine, it reached 763 miles (1,228 kilometers) per hour. *Thrust SSC* was the first car to break the sound barrier (travel faster than the speed of sound).

WHICH IS THE FASTEST BOAT?

Hydroplanes are speedboats that skim over the water, almost as if they are flying. In 1978, Ken Warby roared to 319 miles (514 kilometers) per hour in his jet-powered *Spirit of Australia*. This world record has not yet been broken!

Did you know . . .

In good winds, windsurfers can zip across the water at speeds of more than 50 miles (80 kilometers) per hour.

WHICH ARE THE BIGGEST TIRES?

The world's biggest tires are made for the huge dump trucks that are driven on construction sites. The air-filled tires cushion the trucks' heavy loads of rock, gravel, and earth. The tires may be more than 12 feet (3.6 meters) high—that is about three times as tall as you are!

WHICH IS THE STEEPEST RAILROAD?

Did you know . . .

The world's highest railroad links Tibet to the rest of China. One section, the Tanggula Pass, is more than 16,400 feet (5,000 meters) above sea level.

The view is fantastic on the Katoomba Scenic Railway in Australia's Blue Mountains, but the ride is pretty hairy! The railroad is the world's steepest, dropping 1,362 feet (415 meters) in a little under two minutes. The railroad was built to carry miners down the steep slope, but today, it transports tourists instead—up to 84 at a time.

WHICH VOLCANO HAS BLOWN ITS TOP THE MOST?

Did you know . . .

Some volcanoes erupt continuously. Kilauea in Hawaii has been active since 1983, throwing out 177 cubic feet (5 cubic meters) of lava every second.

On August 27, 1883, the volcanic island of Krakatau in Indonesia exploded with a bang that was heard 3,000 miles (4,800 kilometers) away. It threw rocks 34 miles (55 kilometers) up into the sky and killed almost 36,500 people. Over the next ten days, dust fell as far as 3,300 miles (5,330 kilometers) away.

WHICH MOUNTAINS GROW INTO ISLANDS?

Did you know . . .

The Hawaiian Islands are a string of volcanic islands out in the middle of the Pacific Ocean. The largest island, Hawaii itself, is home to Mauna Loa, the world's tallest volcano.

Thousands of tiny islands dot the world's oceans, and most of them were made by volcanoes slowly growing up from the ocean floor. With each eruption, another layer of cooled lava builds up, until the volcano is tall enough to poke out above the surface.

43

WHICH ARE THE TALLEST CRANES?

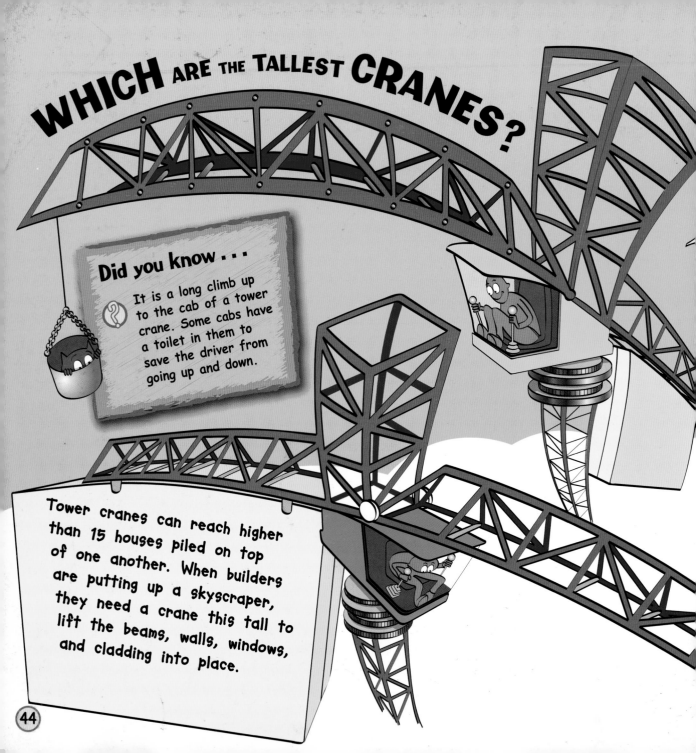

Did you know . . .

It is a long climb up to the cab of a tower crane. Some cabs have a toilet in them to save the driver from going up and down.

Tower cranes can reach higher than 15 houses piled on top of one another. When builders are putting up a skyscraper, they need a crane this tall to lift the beams, walls, windows, and cladding into place.

Did you know . . .

Potala Palace towers above the streets of Lhasa. It is very grand. It has more than 1,000 rooms, and even its roofs are made of gold!

The city of Lhasa is in Tibet, a region of China. Tibet borders the Himalayas, which are the world's highest mountains—so no wonder it is sometimes called the "roof of the world." Lhasa itself is 11,800 feet (3,600 meters) above sea level. It is built among the clouds, which blanket the city in a thick, wet mist.

WHICH ARE THE SMALLEST BOATS?

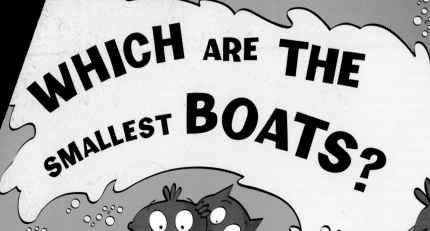

Coracles are just about the world's smallest boats—they usually have room for only one person! Traditionally, these round boats were made from woven grasses, reeds, or saplings and then, sometimes, made waterproof with a coat of tar.

WHICH CONTINENT CONTAINS THE MOST COUNTRIES?

Did you know . . .

The United Nations (UN) has 192 member countries. There are two independent nations—Kosovo and Vatican City—that are not UN members.

Africa contains more countries than any other continent—53 of the world's 194 countries are found there. Many African countries are very new. In 1950, there were only 82 separate countries in the whole world.

WHICH HURRICANE BLEW THE HARDEST?

Did you know . . .

Hurricanes are given a name once their winds exceed 40 miles (65 kilometers) per hour. They are named in alphabetical order, with alternate girls' and boys' names.

The hurricane with the fastest-recorded winds was Hurricane Wilma in 2005. Its top wind speed was 183 miles (295 kilometers) per hour. Wilma killed 23 people. Hurricane Mitch, which struck in 1998, did not blow as hard but caused the deaths of more than 19,000 people.

WHICH IS THE WORLD'S BIGGEST CITY?

Did you know . . .

Every square mile in Tokyo is home to more than 6,700 people. No other city is so packed!

Tokyo, Japan, is the biggest city in the world. More than 36 million people live in Tokyo and its suburbs, with 13 million squashed into the city center. Delhi in India and São Paulo in Brazil are the next two biggest cities. They are each home to more than 20 million people.

WHICH COMPUTER WAS AS BIG AS A BUS?

Did you know . . .

Today's pocket-sized cell phones contain many, many times more computing power than early computers such as Colossus.

The first computer was about as long as four buses and was called Colossus. It was built in the United Kingdom and turned on in 1943. Very few people knew about it at the time because one of its first jobs was to crack secret codes.

WHICH BRIDGE CAN BREAK IN HALF?

London's Tower Bridge carries traffic over the River Thames. The road is built in two halves that can be raised or lowered like drawbridges. When a tall ship sails up the river, each half of the bridge lifts up so that the ship can pass through.

Did you know . . .

Sydney Harbour Bridge, Australia, is the world's widest bridge. Two trains, eight cars, a cyclist, and a person walking a dog can all cross it side by side.

WHICH IS THE BIGGEST INSTRUMENT?

Did you know . . .

The world's most valuable instruments are violins made more than 300 years ago by an Italian named Antonio Stradivari. Buying one costs more than a house!

The organ is the biggest musical instrument. The largest and loudest organ in the world is in Atlantic City, New Jersey. It is so huge that it sounds as loud as 25 brass bands playing together. It has 12 keyboards and more than 33,000 pipes. Sadly, this record-breaking instrument does not work very well these days.

WHICH MOUSE IS MUSICAL?

Did you know . . .

The 18th-century composer Domenico Scarlatti claimed his pet cat helped write his "Cat's Fugue"—when it tiptoed along the keys of his harpsichord.

The male grasshopper mouse of North America uses his shrill chirping song to attract a mate. He stands up on his back legs and sings his heart out. It is his way of telling all of the female mice around what a fine, strong mouse he is.

WHICH COUNTRY HAS MORE SHEEP THAN PEOPLE?

Did you know . . .

India is home to more than one fourth of all of the world's cattle. More than 280 million cows and domestic buffalo live there.

Australia has more sheep than any other country. At the last count, there were 110 million sheep—about five times the number of people. Neighboring New Zealand has few people and around 40 million sheep. In fact, there are ten times more sheep than people in that country!

WHICH IS THE MOST CROWDED COUNTRY?

Monaco in southern Europe is famous for its car racing, but it is also the most crowded country in the world. Its population of 35,400 people is packed into an area of less than 0.78 square miles (2 square kilometers). In comparison, Mongolia in central Asia is one of the emptiest countries. Only 4.4 people live in each square mile there.

Did you know...

The record for the world's smallest country is held by Vatican City in Rome. It is only 0.17 square miles (0.44 square kilometers) in size.

QUICK-QUIZ QUESTIONS

7. Where is the Sahara?

1. Mercury is the hottest planet. True or false?

2. Name a dwarf planet.

8. The Pacific Ocean covers one half of Earth's surface. True or false?

9. Unscramble US VIVE US to find the name of a volcano in Italy.

3. Unscramble RIPEN US ROUSE DAD to get the name of a tiny dinosaur.

4. How much does a coco-de-mer seed weigh?

10. What do decibels measure?

5. Who was the ancient Roman king of the gods?

6. Which planet is home to the solar system's biggest volcano?

11. What is an exoskeleton?

12. Where is Glowworm Grotto?

13. How do chameleons catch their dinner?

14. Which beetle weighs as much as a hamster?

15. When was the first-ever World Cup held?

16. Which American president gave his name to toy bears?

17. How many jet engines did the fastest-ever car have?

18. Who drove the fastest-ever speedboat?

19. Unscramble SAINT SUN DOME AN to find a famous mountain range.

20. What is the name of the largest of the Hawaiian Islands?

21. Where is Potala Palace?

22. What is a coracle?

23. How fast were Hurricane Wilma's winds?

24. Unscramble VARIANT STOOD IN AIR to find the name of a famous violin maker.

25. Which is the world's smallest country?

QUICK-QUIZ ANSWERS

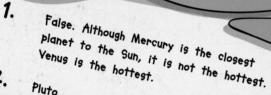

1. False. Although Mercury is the closest planet to the Sun, it is not the hottest. Venus is the hottest.

2. Pluto.

3. RIPEN US ROUSE DAD = Epidendrosaurus.

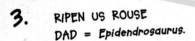

4. Up to 44 pounds (20 kilograms).

5. Jupiter.

6. Mars.

7. It is a desert in North Africa.

8. False. It covers one third of Earth's surface.

9. US VIVE US = Vesuvius.

10. Noise levels.

11. The tough outer skin that protects and supports an invertebrate's body.

12. Waitomo Cave in New Zealand.

13. By shooting out their long, sticky tongue.

14. The Goliath beetle.

15. In 1930.

16. Theodore (Teddy) Roosevelt.

17. Two.

18. Ken Warby.

19. SAINT SUN DOME AN = Andes Mountains.

20. Hawaii.

21. Lhasa, Tibet.

22. A small, round boat.

23. They traveled at up to 183 miles (295 kilometers) per hour.

24. VARIANT STOOD IN AIR = Antonio Stradivari.

25. Vatican City.

TRICKY WORDS

ARCHAEOLOGIST
Someone whose job it is to find out about human history by finding and studying remains such as buildings and clothing.

CLADDING
The outer layer of a building, designed to keep out the weather and make the building look attractive.

COMPOSER
Someone who writes music.

CONTINENT
One of Earth's seven main landmasses—North America, South America, Europe, Africa, Asia, Australia, and Antarctica.

CORACLE
A small, round boat.

CYCAD
A primitive plant with a straight trunk topped by a crown of leathery leaves.

DECIBEL
A unit of measurement that indicates how loud a sound is.

DESERT
A dry region with little plant life.

DRAWBRIDGE
A bridge that is hinged at one end so that it can be raised and lowered.

EGYPTIANS
An ancient people who lived in Egypt, from around 5,000 to 2,000 years ago.

EXOSKELETON
The tough outer skin that protects the soft body of an invertebrate (spineless) animal.

FROND
The leaflike part of seaweeds.

HADROSAUR
A two-legged dinosaur that had a ducklike beak and, usually, a head crest.

HARPSICHORD
A keyboard instrument popular in the 1700s and 1800s.

HURRICANE
A strong storm that forms over warm seas. Its winds travel at 70 miles (120 kilometers) per hour or more.

HYDROPLANE
A fast motorboat that travels just above the water.

INVERTEBRATE
An animal without a backbone (spine).

IRON
A hard, gray metal that reacts with moisture to form iron oxide, or rust.

JET ENGINE
An engine that burns fuel to produce a jet of hot gases that shoots out of the back of the engine, propelling the vehicle forward.

LAVA
Liquid rock that spurts from volcanoes or cracks in Earth's surface.

PATENT
To register an idea or invention with the government so that no one else is allowed to copy it.

PLANET
A large, ball-shaped object in space that orbits (travels around) a star. Earth is a planet.

POACHER
Someone who hunts animals illegally.

POLLEN
Dustlike particles produced by a flower that contain its male sex cells. When pollen brushes against another flower, that flower can produce seeds.

PREDATOR
An animal that hunts and eats other animals.

PREHISTORIC
Describes the period of history before our written records began.

PREY
An animal that is hunted and eaten by other animals.

REDWOOD
An evergreen conifer tree, with reddish timber.

REPTILE
An animal with a backbone and scaly skin. Most reptiles lay eggs on land, but some give birth to live young.

ROMANS
An ancient people from Italy who lived around 2,000 years ago in Europe, Africa, and Asia.

SAUROPOD
A huge, long-necked, plant-eating dinosaur that walked on all fours.

SOLAR SYSTEM
The Sun and the objects in space that orbit it, including the eight planets.

SPEED OF SOUND
How fast sound travels through air—around 768 miles (1,236 kilometers) per hour.

SUBMERSIBLE
A small, underwater craft.

TAIL CLUB
A lumpy mass of bone at the end of an animal's tail, used in self-defense.

TAR
A black, sticky substance from rocks. Tar is used to coat road surfaces and to make boats waterproof.

VOLCANO
A vent (hole) in the surface or crust of a planet through which gas, ash, and molten rock escape. The material that erupts can build up to form a mountain.

WORLD CUP
An international soccer competition that usually takes place every four years.

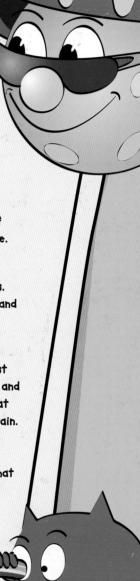

WHERE TO FIND STUFF

Wow! What an amazing
journey! We hope you had
as much fun as we did and learned
many new things. Who knew there was
so much to discover about "WHICH!"
Speaking of "which," here are a few
more exciting books to explore:

The Book of . . . How?
The Book of . . . What?
The Book of . . . Where?
The Book of . . . Who?
The Book of . . . Why?

Look out for these great books!
"Who" knows "what" we'll discover . . .

See you soon!